General Knowledge Olympiad

Class 04

A must have book for all
Olympiads & Talent Search Exams...

by
Deepak Sharma

BLOOM CAP
Bloom Cap Edu Ventures Pvt. Ltd.

Bloom Cap Edu Ventures Pvt. Ltd.

卐 **Administrative & Production Office**

'Ramchhaya' 4577/15, Agarwal Road, Darya Ganj, New Delhi -110002
Tele: 011- 47630600, 43518550

卐 **ISBN :** 978-93-25519-43-5

卐 **PRICE :** ₹100.00

卐 **PO No :** TXT-XX-XXXXXXX-X-XX

For further information about the books log on to
www.bloomcap.org

Follow us on   

Preface

"Future belongs to those Who prepares for it today"

School Olympiads are National & International level competitions conducted by different Government, Non-Government & Educational Organisations with the purpose of making the children ready to face competitive exams.

The challenging Questions asked in Olympiads motivate them to learn more & more and bring out the best result with improved academic performance. The Awards & Scholarship offered by Olympiads motivate children to aspire & strive for doing better and emerge out to be the best.

GK Olympiads

GK is the knowledge of every aspect of the human life, which may or may not be the part of routine academic studies but very important for the overall personality development of the students. It is more or less connected with the attentiveness and awareness. There can be different domains of GK like; History, Geography, Polity, Culture, Discovery, Sports, Current Affairs etc.

GK Olympiads help students in understanding the importance of General Knowledge and updations about National & International Affairs in daily life..

'Bloom GK Olympiad Study Book Class 4' is a perfect resource to Study & Practice for Olympiad Exams and other National & State Level Talent Search Exams & Other Competitions.

Some Special Features of Bloom GK Olympiad Study Books are;

- Complete coverage of all the topics related to GK;. Geography, Environment, Polity, Culture, Sports, etc.
- Chapterwise Exercises having different types of Objective Questions.
- Olympiad Pattern Practice Sets at the end.

This book is prepared by Expert Panel with the utmost care, still if you have any suggestions regarding its improvement then feel free to contact us at olympiads@bloomcap.org. We will try to inculcate your suggestions in the further editions.

Contents

Chapter 01

Solar System

1. Who discovered that the Earth revolves around the Sun?
   (a) Galileo Galilei　　　　　　　　(b) Isaac Newton
   (c) Albert Einstein　　　　　　　　(d) Kepler

2. The planets with no moons is/are ....
   (a) Venus and Mars　　　　　　　　(b) Mars and Neptune
   (c) Mercury and Mars　　　　　　　(d) Mercury and Venus

3. I am the largest member of the Solar System. I have my own light and without my light plants can't manufacture its food. Who am I?
   (a) Earth　　　　　　　　　　　　　(b) Jupiter
   (c) Sun　　　　　　　　　　　　　　(d) Saturn

4. The Earth rotates in the direction ....
   (a) East to West　　　　　　　　　(b) North to South
   (c) South to North　　　　　　　　(d) West to East

5. Which of the following is/are true about Sun?
   (a) It is made up of gases　　　　(b) It has its own heat and light
   (c) Sun is a star　　　　　　　　　(d) All of these

6. Which among the following is called a 'Dwarf planet'?
   (a) Saturn　　　　　　　　　　　　(b) Jupiter
   (c) Mars　　　　　　　　　　　　　(d) Pluto

7. If there is no Sun in the sky, the colour of the sky would be ....
   (a) blue　　　　　　　　　　　　　(b) orange
   (c) black　　　　　　　　　　　　　(d) green

8. How many planets of the Solar System have rings?
   (a) 1　　　　　　　　　　　　　　　(b) 2
   (c) 6　　　　　　　　　　　　　　　(d) 4

9. In the .... season, the Earth is closest to the Sun.
   (a) Summer   (b) Winter
   (c) Spring   (d) Autumn

10. Which of the following is a terrestrial planet?
    (a) Jupiter   (b) Venus
    (c) Neptune   (d) Uranus

11. Which is the farthest planet from the Sun?
    (a) Uranus   (b) Jupiter
    (c) Mercury   (d) Neptune

12. Why do astronauts wear oxygen mask on Moon?
    (a) There is no atmosphere or oxygen on Moon to breathe.
    (b) To avoid suffocation after a long flight in spacecraft.
    (c) To be used in case of emergency.
    (d) None of the above

13. The planet with the highest number of Moons is ....
    (a) Saturn   (b) Jupiter
    (c) Neptune   (d) Uranus

14. Titan is one of the Moon of ....
    (a) Jupiter   (b) Saturn
    (c) Venus   (d) Earth

15. The imaginary line dividing the Earth in two halves is called an ....
    (a) Equator   (b) Half line
    (c) Orbit   (d) Path

16. The lightest planet of our Solar System is ....
    (a) Saturn   (b) Earth
    (c) Neptune   (d) Mars

17. A piece of stone and/or iron travelling through space that moves through the Earth's atmosphere is ....
    (a) Planet   (b) Sun
    (c) Moon   (d) Meteor

18. The path Earth moves around the Sun is called the ....
    (a) Axis   (b) Rotation
    (c) Counterclockwise   (d) Orbit

19. The Moon .... the Sun's light.
    (a) hides   (b) reflects
    (c) loses   (d) absorbs

20. In how many days Moon complete one revolution around the Earth?
(a) 29 days   (b) 30 days
(c) 27 days   (d) 25 days

21. Sun looks bigger and brighter than other stars, for which one of the following reasons?
(a) Because it is big ball of fire.   (b) Because it is far away from us.
(c) Because it is the closest star to us.   (d) Because it is a young star.

22. Consider the following statements and answer correctly from the options given below.
Statement 1 Meteors are shooting stars which can be seen during Night.
Statement 2 Milky Way galaxy is made up of millions of stars.
Codes
(a) 1 is incorrect and 2 is correct   (b) 1 is correct and 2 is incorrect
(c) Both 1 and 2 are correct   (d) Both 1 and 2 are incorrect

23. About how long does it take the Moon to complete a full lunar cycle?
(a) One year   (b) One month
(c) One week   (d) One day

24. Which of the given statements is/are corect?
Statement 1 Earth's Moon is the largest satellite of solar system.
Statement 2 Size of Moon is smaller than Earth's size.
Codes
(a) Both statements are correct   (b) Only 1 is correct
(c) Only 2 is correct   (d) None of the statements are correct

25. Why there is no life on the Moon?
(a) Because Moon is a natural satellite of the Earth.
(b) Because there are huge holes on the Moon called craters.
(c) Because it does not have its own light.
(d) Because there is no water or air on the Moon.

26. Which of the given statements is/are correct?
Statement 1 Sun is made up of Hydrogen and Helium Gas.
Statement 2 Seasons are caused on Earth due to its revolution around Sun.
Codes
(a) Both 1 and 2 are correct   (b) Only 1 is correct
(c) Only 2 is correct   (d) None of the statements are correct

27. Which of the following objects is capable of producing its own natural light?
(a) The Sun   (b) Our Moon
(c) Earth   (d) A planet

28. When does a lunar eclipse occur?
  (a) When the Earth is between the Sun and the Moon.
  (b) When the Moon is between Earth and Sun.
  (c) When the Sun is between Earth and Moon.
  (d) None of the above

29. Which of the following provides energy to plants to make food?
  (a) Moon   (b) Water
  (c) Sun   (d) Soil

30. What causes the Sun to rise and set every day?
  (a) The orbit of Earth
  (b) The rotation of Earth
  (c) The revolution of Earth
  (d) The apparent movement of Earth

Chapter 02

My Country

1. Which city is known as the city of seven Islands?
   (a) Pune
   (b) Chennai
   (c) Mumbai
   (d) Dwarka

2. Port Blair is the capital of which Union Territory?
   (a) Andaman and Nicobar Islands
   (b) Daman and Diu
   (c) Puducherry
   (d) None of these

3. Which of the following is not a Union Territory?
   (a) Ladakh
   (b) Chandigarh
   (c) Jammu and Kashmir
   (d) Sikkim

4. The capital of Goa is ....
   (a) Imphal
   (b) Itanagar
   (c) Hyderabad
   (d) Panaji

5. Which of the following city is not situated near or on the bank of river Ganga?
   (a) Delhi
   (b) Varanasi
   (c) Kolkata
   (d) Haridwar

6. Gandhinagar is the capital of which state?
   (a) Gujarat
   (b) Maharashtra
   (c) Telangana
   (d) Goa

7. The National War Memorial is a monument built by the Government of India in .... to honour the Indian Armed Forces.
   (a) Mumbai
   (b) Amritsar
   (c) New Delhi
   (d) Bengaluru

8. The cities of Banglore and Mysore are located in which state?
   (a) Bihar
   (b) Uttar Pradesh
   (c) Karnataka
   (d) Goa

9. Which city is known as Blue City or Sun City of India?
   (a) Jaisalmer   (b) Delhi   (c) Lucknow   (d) Jodhpur

10. Which of the following city is located in South India?
    (a) Amritsar   (b) Kolkata
    (c) Hyderabad   (d) Varanasi

11. Which city is known as the Diamond city of India?
    (a) Hathras   (b) Jaisalmer   (c) Surat   (d) Pune

12. Itanagar is the capital of ....
    (a) Bihar   (b) Goa
    (c) Chhattisgarh   (d) Arunachal Pradesh

13. The hill stations Manali and Shimla are located in which state?
    (a) Tamil Nadu   (b) Punjab
    (c) Uttarakhand   (d) Himachal Pradesh

14. Name the largest state (of India) in terms of population.
    (a) Uttarakhand   (b) Uttar Pradesh
    (c) West Bengal   (d) Maharashtra

15. Which city of India is known as Silk city of India?
    (a) Jaipur   (b) Pochampally
    (c) Udaipur   (d) Kanpur

16. Dispur is the capital city of which North-Eastern state?
    (a) Assam   (b) Tripura
    (c) Meghalaya   (d) Mizoram

17. Kavaratti is the capital of which Union Territory?
    (a) Daman and Diu   (b) Lakshadweep
    (c) Dadar and Nagar Haveli   (d) Chandigarh

18. .... is the capital of Madhya Pradesh.
    (a) Gwalior   (b) Bhopal   (c) Ujjain   (d) Indore

19. Which of the given pairs are matched correctly?

Famous Place		City
A. Dal Lake	—	Srinagar
B. Rock Garden	—	Chandigarh
C. Old Fort	—	Mumbai

Codes
(a) A and B   (b) A and C
(c) A and B   (d) All of these

20. Which city was earlier known as Madras?
(a) Mumbai   (b) Chennai   (c) Kolkata   (d) Patna

21. Which city is known as the Steel city of India?
(a) Shilong   (b) Durgapur   (c) Jamshedpur   (d) Cuttack

22. .... is the capital of Punjab.
(a) Delhi   (b) Jaipur   (c) Chandigarh   (d) Chennai

23. Which of the given pairs are correctly matched?

	City		State
A.	Pune	—	Maharashtra
B.	Ajmer	—	Rajasthan
C.	Patiala	—	Haryana

Codes

(a) B and C   (b) A and C

(c) A and B   (d) All of these

24. Kanchenjunga mountain is located in........... .
(a) Himachal Pradesh   (b) Jammu and Kashmir
(c) Ladakh   (d) Sikkim

25. Match List I with List II.

List I (State)		List II (Capital)
A. Jharkhand	1.	Shillong
B. Odisha	2.	Thiruvananthapuram
C. Meghalaya	3.	Ranchi
D. Kerala	4.	Bhubaneswar

Codes

	A	B	C	D		A	B	C	D
(a)	1	3	2	4	(b)	3	4	1	2
(c)	4	1	2	3	(d)	4	3	2	1

Famous Buildings and Monuments

1. Name the place where Jagannath temple is situated.
   (a) Tamil Nadu
   (b) Uttar Pradesh
   (c) Haryana
   (d) Odisha

2. Where is Ajanta and Ellora caves are located?
   (a) Odisha
   (b) Telangana
   (c) Maharashtra
   (d) Karnataka

3. The monument shown in the image given below is ....

   (a) Sun temple
   (b) Agra Fort
   (c) Gol Gumbaz
   (d) Sanchi Stupa

4. What was built by emperor Shah Jahan when he shifted his capital from Agra to Delhi?
   (a) Taj Mahal
   (b) Qutub Minar
   (c) Red Fort
   (d) Sanchi

5. Badrinath is situated on the bank of river ....
   (a) Krishna
   (b) Yamuna
   (c) Alaknanda
   (d) Sarasvati

6. Jantar Mantar is located in which other city, apart from Delhi?
   (a) Mumbai
   (b) Jaipur
   (c) Chennai
   (d) Bhopal

7. Which was a centre of learning and a Buddhist monastery from 3rd century BC to the 13th century CE?
   (a) Red Fort   (b) Qutub Minar
   (c) Jantar Mantar   (d) Nalanda

8. Fatehpur Sikri is located in ....
   (a) Uttarakhand   (b) Uttar Pradesh
   (c) Jharkhand   (d) Rajasthan

9. The world famous 'Khajuraho' sculptures are located in.................. .
   (a) Gujarat   (b) Madhya Pradesh
   (c) Odisha   (d) Maharashtra

10. Where is Gol-Gumbaz located?

   (a) Telangana   (b) Rajasthan
   (c) Maharashtra   (d) Karnataka

11. What is Jantar Mantar?
    (a) An Astronomical Observatory   (b) A Museum
    (c) A Fort   (d) A Mughal Garden

12. Which monument was built to commemorate the visit of King George V and Queen Mary to Bombay?
    (a) India Gate   (b) Gateway of India
    (c) Victoria Terminus   (d) Elephanta Caves

13. Which is the most holy pilgrimage spot of the Buddhism?
    (a) Khajuraho   (b) Bodh Gaya
    (c) Ajanta   (d) Ellora

14. Where is Dargah of Khwaja Moinuddin Chishti is located?
    (a) Ajmer   (b) Udaipur
    (c) Jaisalmer   (d) Pushkar

15. In which city famous Sun temple is located?

(a) Varanasi   (b) Mathura   (c) Konark   (d) Gorakhpur

16. Name the place where Sri Ranganathaswamy Temple is located.

(a) Tiruchirappalli   (b) Delhi

(c) Pune   (d) Nagpur

17. Name the tomb shown in the image.

Hint : It is situated in Maharashtra and it is known as Taj of Deccan.

(a) Safdarjung's Tomb   (b) Amer Fort

(c) Bibi Ka Maqbara   (d) Diwan-i-Aam

18. Identify the temple shown in the image, it is situated in Madurai, Tamil Nadu.

(a) Meenakshi Amman Temple   (b) Shree Somnath Jyotirlinga Temple

(c) Yogmaya Temple   (d) None of these

19. Identify the statue shown in the image , it is situated in 'Rio de Janeiro', Brazil.

(a) Christ the Redeemer (b) St. Peter Statue
(c) Statue of Liberty (d) St. Michel Statue

20. The Colosseum is located in which country?
(a) Italy (b) France
(c) Norway (d) Germany

21. The famous Pyramids of Giza are located in which country?
(a) Algeria (b) Lebanon
(c) Egypt (d) Iraq

22. St. Basil's Cathedral is located in which country?

(a) Mongolia (b) Greece
(c) Turkey (d) Russia

23. Burj Al Arab is located in which country?

(a) Bahrain   (b) Kuwait
(c) United Kingdom   (d) Saudi Arabia

24. Mecca, the holy site of Muslims is located in which country?
(a) Saudi Arabia   (b) Oman
(c) Kuwait   (d) Bahrain

25. Identify the building shown in the image, it is headquater of British monarch and located in Westminster, London.

(a) Buckingham Palace   (b) White House
(c) Summer Palace   (d) Mysore Palace

Our Culture

1. The oldest Indian language is..................... .
   (a) Marathi (b) Punjabi
   (c) Tamil (d) Hindi

2. Which is the Rajasthani dance that is performed by women by carrying earthen pots on their heads?
   (a) Raika (b) Tera Tali
   (c) Panihari (d) Suisini

3. The dance shown in the image given below is..................... .

   (a) Dandiya Dance (b) Ghumar Dance
   (c) Bihu Dance (d) Kuchipudi

4. 'Madhubani', a style of folk paintings, is popular in which of the following states in India?
   (a) Uttar Pradesh (b) Rajasthan
   (c) Madhya Pradesh (d) Bihar

5. Which among the following is a folk dance of India?
   (a) Garba (b) Kathakali
   (c) Manipuri (d) Mohiniattam

6. Which among the following temples of India is known as 'Black Pagoda'?
   (a) Brihadeeshwara Temple, Tanjore (b) Sun Temple, Konark
   (c) Meenakshi Temple, Madurai (d) Jagannath Temple, Puri

7. How many languages are mentioned on the Indian currency note?
   (a) 20   (b) 25   (c) 22   (d) 15

8. Which of the following festival is celebrated in Nagaland every year?
   (a) Carnival   (b) Ugadi
   (c) Hornbill   (d) Puram

9. Which classical dance is famous in Tamil Nadu?
   (a) Kuchipudi   (b) Mohiniyattam
   (c) Bharatanatyam   (d) Kathakali

10. In which of the following states of India, Yakshagana, a dance drama is popular?
    (a) Tamil Nadu   (b) Karnataka
    (c) Kerala   (d) Madhya Pradesh

11. Dogari is a language of ....
    (a) Nagaland   (b) Jammu and Kashmir
    (c) Odisha   (d) West Bengal

12. Identify the famous Indian festival with the help of given information.
    1. The festival is celebrated in the month of August and September.
    2. It is a harvest festival.
    (a) Pongal   (b) Onam
    (c) Mudiyettu   (d) Bhogi

13. Which of the given statements are true?
    Statement 1 Madhubani paintings is famous art form of Bihar.
    Statement 2 Warli paintings are famous in Maharashtra and Gujarat.
    Codes
    (a) Only 1 is true   (b) Only 2 is true
    (c) Both are true   (d) None of the statements are true

14. Which of the following statement is true?
    Statement 1 The Ancient name of city of Varanasi was Kashi.
    Statement 2 Ahmedabad is a heritage city of India.
    Codes
    (a) Only 1 is true   (b) Only 2 is true
    (c) Both are true   (d) None of the statements are true

15. The language with richest vocabulary is ....
    (a) Hindi   (b) German   (c) French   (d) English

16. Birju Maharaj is famous for which form of dance ?
    (a) Kathak   (b) Bharatanatyam
    (c) Manipuri   (d) Kuchipudi

17. Which is the oldest religious text found in India?
    (a) Ramayana   (b) Mahabharata
    (c) Gita   (d) Rigveda

18. Konkani is a language of ....
    (a) Kerala   (b) Karnataka
    (c) Goa   (d) Assam

19. Which is the official language of Assam?
    (a) Assamese   (b) Hindi
    (c) Asom   (d) Dogri

20. Which festival is celebrated by flying colourful kites in the sky?

    (a) Lohri   (b) Dusshera
    (c) Bihu   (d) Makar Sankranti

21. To which state does the Sattriya dance belong?
    (a) Mizoram   (b) Manipur
    (c) Assam   (d) Meghalaya

22. Rouff is a folk dance. It has its origin in ....

    (a) Assam   (b) Mizoram
    (c) Kashmir   (d) Himachal Pradesh

23. Dance patterns considered sacred to Lord Shiva are in............
    (a) Bharatanatyam and Kathakali   (b) Kathak and Bharatanatyam
    (c) Bharatanatyam and Mohiniyattam   (d) Oddissi and Bharatanatyam

Capital and Currencies

1. Abu Dhabi is the capital city of which country?
   (a) Iran
   (b) Iraq
   (c) Mauritius
   (d) United Arab Emirates

2. What is the capital of Iran?
   (a) Tehran
   (b) Tabriz
   (c) Shiraz
   (d) Isfahan

3. The national currency of Bangladesh is ....
   (a) Lek
   (b) Slotty
   (c) Taka
   (d) None of these

4. What is the capital city of Italy which is also referred to as the "Eternal City" of the world?
   (a) Rome
   (b) Washington DC
   (c) Tripoli
   (d) Skopje

5. Amsterdam is the capital city of which country?
   (a) Nepal
   (b) New Zealand
   (c) Netherlands
   (d) Myanmar

6. What is the national currency of Germany?
   (a) Naira
   (b) Euro
   (c) Rupee
   (d) Pound

7. The national currency of Sri Lanka is ....
   (a) Rupee
   (b) Baht
   (c) Pound
   (d) Lira

8. Which of the following is the capital of Egypt?
   (a) Islamabad
   (b) Cairo
   (c) Kathmandu
   (d) None of these

9. What is the capital of Bhutan?
   (a) Paro   (b) Mongar   (c) Thimphu   (d) Jakar

10. What is the capital of Canada?
    (a) Toronto   (b) Ottawa
    (c) Santiago   (d) None of these

11. The national currency of Australia is ....
    (a) Rupiah   (b) Yen   (c) Dollar   (d) Yuan

12. Wellington is the capital of which country?
    (a) New Zealand   (b) United States of America (USA)
    (c) Kenya   (d) None of these

13. Which of the following country is the most populous country?
    (a) Indonesia   (b) United States of America
    (c) India   (d) China

14. What is the capital city of the Philippines?
    (a) Warsaw   (b) Quezon City
    (c) Manila   (d) Davao City

15. Match List I with List II.

	List I		List II
A.	China	1.	Kathmandu
B.	Nepal	2.	Islamabad
C.	Pakistan	3.	New Delhi
D.	India	4.	Beijing

Codes

	A	B	C	D		A	B	C	D
(a)	4	3	2	1	(b)	3	2	4	1
(c)	2	3	1	4	(d)	4	1	2	3

16. What is the capital of Bangladesh?
    (a) Madaripur   (b) Dhaka
    (c) Khulna   (d) Barishal

17. Which country is known as the land of rising Sun?
    (a) Japan   (b) India
    (c) Australia   (d) Pakistan

18. Mount Fuji is located in ....
(a) USA
(b) Japan
(c) Indonesia
(d) Greece

19. The national currency of Malaysia is ....
(a) Lira
(b) Dollar
(c) Kwacha
(d) Ringgit

20. What is the largest country in the world in terms of land area?
(a) Russia
(b) Canada
(c) USA
(d) China

21. Name the currency shown in the image.

(a) Yuan
(b) Dinar
(c) Rupees
(d) None of these

22. Which of the following is the currency of Japan?
(a) Yen
(b) Dollar
(c) Pound
(d) Dinar

23. Kabul is capital of which country?
(a) Bangladesh
(b) India
(c) Afghanistan
(d) None of these

24. Find the incorrect pair of Countries and Capitals given below.
(a) Italy-Rome
(b) Kuwait-Kuwait City
(c) Nepal-Kathmandu
(d) South Korea-Moscow

25. The currency of which country has the image of Benjamin Franklin?
(a) Australia
(b) Canada
(c) United States of America
(d) Germany

International Personalities

1. Who is the father of Geometry?
   (a) Aristotle
   (b) Euclid
   (c) Pythagoras
   (d) Kepler

2. Identify the personality shown in the image.

   (a) Martin Luther King
   (b) Barack Obama
   (c) Abraham Lincoln
   (d) Winston Churchill

3. The personality shown in the image is the founder of which company?

   (a) Facebook
   (b) Microsoft
   (c) Dell
   (d) Infosys

4. Identify the person shown in the image.

(a) Adolf Hitler
(b) Martin Luther King
(c) Karl Marx
(d) None of these

5. .... is the first person and the only woman to win the Nobel Prize twice, and the only person to win the Nobel Prize in two scientific fields.
(a) Maria Goeppert Mayer
(b) Marie Curie
(c) Dorothy Hodgkin
(d) Barbara McClintock

6. Who is the great scientist shown in the image given below?

(a) Albert Einstein   (b) Thomas Edison   (c) Stephen Hawking   (d) Nikola Tesla

7. Who among the following is the former President of South Africa?
(a) Nelson Mandela
(b) Barack Obama
(c) Boris Johnson
(d) Steve Biko

8. Who is the founder of google?
(a) Jeff Bezos
(b) Hilary Clinton
(c) Larry Page and Sergy Brin
(d) Mark Zukerberg

9. Who among the following is known as 'American Gandhi'?
(a) Barack Obama
(b) Donald Trump
(c) Martin Luther King
(d) Joe Biden

10. Name the first women Vice-President of America.
(a) Rihana
(b) Lady Gaga
(c) Kamla Harris
(d) Margaret Thatcher

11. Steve Jobs and Steve Wozniak are the founder of which multinational company?
(a) Apple (b) Microsoft (c) Adobe (d) Samsung

12. Identify the person shown in the image.

(a) Jeff Bezos (b) Bill Gates (c) Mukesh Ambani (d) Donald Trump

13. Who is the founder of Facebook?
(a) Mark Zukerberg (b) Bill Gates (c) Elon Musk (d) None of these

14. Who is the personality shown in the image given below?

(a) Queen Victoria (b) Queen Elizabeth
(c) Sheikh Hasina (d) Aung Sang Syu Ki

15. Identify the person shown in the image.

(a) Satya Nadela (b) Ratan Tata (c) Satya Narayan Murthy (d) Sundar Pichai

16. Name the youngest Nobel Prize awardee.
    (a) Malala Yousafzai   (b) Marie Curie
    (c) Albert Einstein   (d) None of these

17. Name the artist who made the world famous painting 'Mona Lisa'.
    (a) M.F. Hussain   (b) Leonardo da Vinci
    (c) Pablo Picasso   (d) Jennifer Lopez

18. Which player is also known as 'Lightning Bolt'?
    (a) Usain Bolt   (b) Tiger Woods
    (c) Cristiano Ronaldo   (d) None of these

19. Who is the founder of Microsoft?
    (a) Bill Gates   (b) Jeff Bezos
    (c) Elon Musk   (d) Mark Zukerberg

20. Identify the person shown in the image.

    (a) Baba Ramdev   (b) Dalai Lama
    (c) Morari Bapu   (d) Balkrishna

Our Environment

1. The natural place of an organism or community is known as.......... .
   (a) Niche　　　　　(b) Biome　　　　　(c) Habitat　　　　　(d) Habit

2. Smog is derived from ....
   (a) smoke　　　　　(b) fog　　　　　(c) Only (a)　　　　　(d) Both (a) and (b)

3. .... is the major raw material for biogas.
   (a) Plant leaves　　　　　　　　　(b) Cow dung
   (c) Coal　　　　　　　　　　　　(d) Uranium

4. Find the correct food chain from the following options.
   (a) Deer ------- Lion ------ Snake　　　　(b) Grass ------ Deer ------ Lion
   (c) Grass ------ Lion ------ Deer　　　　(d) Deer ------ Grass ------ Lion

5. Which of the following will cause water pollution?
   (a) Using excessive fertilisers in the field.
   (b) Using recycled waste water for cleaning.
   (c) Putting unwanted waste in abandoned field.
   (d) Both (a) and (c)

6. Which of the following is a cause of acid rain?
   (a) Volcanic eruption　　　　　　　(b) Burning of fossil fuels
   (c) Releasing of smoke from factories　　(d) All of these

7. The Biosphere on Earth includes, which of the following?

   1. Atmosphere　　　2. Hydrosphere　　　3. Lithosphere

   Codes
   (a) Only 1 and 2　　　　　　　　(b) Only 1 and 3
   (c) Only 2 and 3　　　　　　　　(d) All of these

8. Which of the following is not a fossil fuel?
   (a) Coal　　　　　　　　　　　(b) Petroleum
   (c) Natural Gas　　　　　　　　(d) Uranium

9. What are the major factors behind water pollution?
   (a) Oil refineries
   (b) Paper factories
   (c) Sugar mills
   (d) All of these

10. Which of the following is not a green house gas?
    (a) Carbon dioxide
    (b) Methane
    (c) Nitrous oxide
    (d) Carbon monoxide

11. Chlorofluorocarbon is used in............ .
    (a) refrigerators
    (b) air conditioners
    (c) perfumes
    (d) All of these

12. The Gir National Park and Wild Life Sanctuary is located in ....
    (a) Madhya Pradesh
    (b) Gujarat
    (c) Rajasthan
    (d) Uttar Pradesh

13. Which of the following statement is correct?
    1. Nitrogen gas is the most abundant gas in Earth's atmosphere
    2. Carbon dioxide gas is responsible for Global Warming.
    Codes
    (a) Only 1
    (b) Only 2
    (c) Both 1 and 2
    (d) None of these

14. The name of India derived from which river?
    (a) Indus river
    (b) Ganges river
    (c) Brahmaputra river
    (d) Sutlej river

15. The symbol shown in the image represent ....

    (a) Compost
    (b) Recycling
    (c) Biodegradable waste
    (d) Acid rain

16. Which of the following is responsible for turning Taj Mahal yellow?
    (a) Nitrogen dioxide
    (b) Sulphur
    (c) Chlorine
    (d) Sulphur dioxide

17. Where does the energy start in this food chain?

(a) Plant   (b) Sun   (c) Deer   (d) Wolf

18. Which one of the following is a biotic component of the environment?
(a) Water   (b) Air   (c) Land   (d) Plant

19. We, human beings, depend on our .... for all our needs.
(a) atmosphere   (b) environment
(c) lithosphere   (d) hydrosphere

20. The process of gradual increase in the earth's temperature is called ....
(a) Pollution   (b) Green house effect
(c) Global warming   (d) Acid rain

21. Acid rain causes damage to ....
(a) animals life   (b) plants life
(c) historical monuments   (d) All of these

22. Contamination through unwanted substances into water is called ....
(a) Air pollution   (b) Water pollution
(c) Land pollution   (d) Soil pollution

23. The network of drainage pipes to carry waste water is called................ .
(a) Sewer system   (b) Drainage
(c) Water supply system   (d) Waste water supply

24. Burning of dried leaves and other parts of plant causes................ .
(a) air pollution   (b) soil pollution
(c) water pollution   (d) lots of heat is generated

25. Which one is a good habit?
(a) Using plastic bag   (b) Using scooter for short distance
(c) Throwing garbage into drain   (d) Carrying a cloth bag for vegetables

Chapter 08

Human Body

1. The food pipe transports food from the mouth to the stomach. What is the other name of food pipe?
   (a) Duodenum
   (c) Appendix
   (c) Oesophagus
   (d) Pancreas

2. Which of the following protects the nerves which connect brain to other body parts?
   (a) Kidney
   (b) Spine
   (c) Liver
   (d) Ribcage

3. What is the outermost part of the tooth called?
   (a) Dentine
   (b) Enamel
   (c) Pulp
   (d) None of these

4. Which of the following is correct regarding the person who is suffering from cardiac problem?
   (a) He is having problem in his eyes.
   (b) He is having problem in his legs.
   (c) He is having problem in his heart.
   (d) He is having problem in his lungs.

5. Where do most of the nutrients get absorbed in the body?
   (a) Mouth
   (b) Stomach
   (c) Large intestine
   (d) Small intestine

6. If a child of 3-4 years has milk teeth, what kind of tooth he does not have?
   (a) Incisors
   (b) Canines
   (c) Molars
   (d) Premolars

7. Which system includes the brain and spinal cord?
   (a) Nervous System
   (b) Respiratory System
   (c) Muscular System
   (d) Digestive System

8. The blood flows to different parts through ....
   (a) pipes
   (b) blood vessels
   (c) taps
   (d) None of these

9. Pick an excretory organ from the following
   (a) Nose   (b) Hair
   (c) Eyes   (d) Kidneys

10. Ram is watching a movie on television. Which of the following senses is he using?
    (a) Smell and hearing   (b) Touch and smell
    (c) Touch and sight   (d) Sight and hearing

11. Which of the following systems protects our body against diseases and infections?
    (a) Excretory system   (b) Digestive system
    (c) Immune system   (d) Circulatory system

12. Which system does heart belong to?
    (a) Digestive system   (b) Respiratory system
    (c) Circulatory system   (d) Excretory system

13. What does our body provide to fight against diseases?
    (a) Blood   (b) Antibodies
    (c) Weapons   (d) Knife

14. Which of the given statement is correct?

    Statement 1 The blood supplies nutrients to all the body parts.

    Statement 2 The kidney remove waste products from our body.
    Codes
    (a) Only 1   (b) Only 2
    (c) Both 1 and 2   (d) None of these

15. Which organ of our body belongs to both the respiratory and excretory system?
    (a) Lungs   (b) Skin
    (c) Kidneys   (d) Intestine

16. Match List I with List II.

List I	List II
A. Incisors	1. grinding teeth
B. Canines	2. cracking teeth
C. Premolars	3. cutting teeth
D. Molars	4. tearing teeth

Codes

	A	B	C	D			A	B	C	D
(a)	3	4	2	1		(b)	1	2	3	4
(c)	2	3	4	1		(d)	4	3	2	1

17. Which of the following is specialised for filtering water from blood?
    (a) Heart
    (b) Lung
    (c) Liver
    (d) Kidney

18. Which one of the following have no role in digestion of food?
    (a) Liver
    (b) Gall bladder
    (c) Stomach
    (d) Kidney

19. Which of the given pairs are matched correctly?

Food		Nutrient
A. Banana	—	Fat
B. Beans	—	Protein
C. Fish	—	Carbohydrate

Codes
    (a) Only 1
    (b) Only 2
    (c) Only 1 and 2
    (d) All of these

20. Human body is made up of different body parts are called ....
    (a) Mouth
    (b) Organs
    (c) Skin
    (d) Heart

21. Which of the following is an external body organ?
    (a) Ears
    (b) Kidney
    (c) Lung
    (d) Heart

22. Which part of digestive system is shown in the image?

    (a) Small intestine
    (b) Stomach
    (c) Lung
    (d) Rectum

23. The main function of heart is to ....
    (a) pump the blood to all parts of body
    (b) control the body
    (c) remove urea from body
    (d) purify the blood

24. Which of the following sense organs is used to balance our body when we walk?
    (a) Eyes
    (b) Nose
    (c) Ear
    (d) Skin

25. Which mineral is essential for strong bone and teeth?
(a) Iron (b) Calcium
(c) Mercury (d) Iodine

26. The food we eat is stored inside our ....
(a) blood (b) stomach
(c) small intestine (d) kidney

27. Match List I with List II.

List I	List II
A. Controls our actions	1. Excretory system
B. Supplies oxygen to all parts of the body	2. Circulatory system
C. Removes wastes from the body	3. Nervous system
D. Molars	4. Tearing teeth

Codes

	A	B	C	D			A	B	C	D
(a)	3	2	1	4		(b)	2	3	1	4
(c)	1	3	2	4		(d)	None of these			

28. Chewing of food helps in ....
(a) Respiration (b) Digestion
(c) Photosynthesis (d) Reproduction

29. Which vitamin is essential for carrying out repairing of cells in the body?
(a) Vitamin K (b) Vitamin D
(c) Vitamin C (d) Vitamin E

30. Which is the smallest bone of human body?
(a) Stapes (bone of ear) (b) Skull
(c) Ribs (d) Femur

31. Which cells of blood helps in clot formation in case of a cut on the skin?
(a) WBC (b) RBC
(c) Plasma (d) Platelet

Chapter 09

Everyday Science

1. The bubbles that come out rapidly when we open soda water bottle are ....
   - (a) Nitrogen bubbles
   - (b) Oxygen bubbles.
   - (c) Water bubbles
   - (d) Carbon dioxide bubbles

2. The bells used in Temples and Church are made up of which metals?
   - (a) Copper and silver
   - (b) Copper and gold
   - (c) Copper and tin
   - (d) Copper and aluminium

3. Which of the following helps in chewing of food?
   - (a) Tongue
   - (b) Teeth
   - (c) Mouth
   - (d) None of these

4. Why do wooden blocks float on water?
   - (a) Because they are less denser than water.
   - (b) Because they are more denser than water.
   - (c) Because we can make boat of wood.
   - (d) None of these

5. Identify the substance that does not get dissolved in water.
   - (a) Sand
   - (b) Oxygen
   - (c) Water
   - (d) Sugar

6. A mixture of two metals is called an ....
   - (a) Alloy
   - (b) Mixture
   - (c) Solution
   - (d) All of these

7. Which of the following is used in the manufacturing of soaps?
   - (a) Vegetable oil
   - (b) Mobil oil
   - (c) Kerosene oil
   - (d) Petrol

8. Ankur has two glasses. One glass is filled with ice cubes and the other is filled with water. Which of the following shows that ice is different from water?
   - (a) The glass with ice cubes is colder than that with water.
   - (b) Water is liquid and the ice cubes are solid.
   - (c) Water fills more of the glass than ice cubes.
   - (d) All of the above

9. Which of the following materials allow electricity to pass through it?
(a) Plastic
(b) Wood
(c) Silver
(d) All of these

10. The change of a substance from the liquid state to the gaseous state is called
(a) Evaporation
(b) Condensation
(c) Sublimation
(d) Filtration

11. Dark rain clouds can give out lightning and ....
(a) thunder
(b) snow
(c) sunlight
(d) wind

12. What part of the plant conducts Photosynthesis?
(a) Branch
(b) Leaf
(c) Root
(d) Trunk

13. Magnets can be made up of which object?
(a) Wood
(b) Glass
(c) Iron
(d) Plastic

14. Which tissue connects muscles to bones?
(a) Skin
(b) Blood vessels
(c) Fat
(d) Tendon

15. Name the metal that is commonly used in electrical wire.
(a) Iron
(b) Gold
(c) Copper
(d) None of these

16. Rusting of iron takes place in the presence of ....
(a) air and water
(b) air and paint
(c) water and salt
(d) salt and air

17. The burning of fire needs ....
(a) oxygen
(b) carbon dioxide
(c) nitrogen
(d) water vapour

18. The unit of weight for diamonds and other gems is known as ....
(a) Carat
(b) Kg
(c) Litre
(d) Celcius

19. Why does a hydrogen ballon rises in the air?
(a) Because it is lighter than the body of the air which it displaces.
(b) Because it is heavier than the body of the air which it displaces.
(c) Because it has bigger shape than air.
(d) All of the above

20. Which of the following technology is used to make modern-day televisions?
(a) ATM
(b) LED
(c) DVD
(d) LTE

Computers

1. Which of the following is not a pointing device?
   (a) Keyboard (b) Mouse
   (c) Joystick (d) Light pen

2. On which menu are cut, copy and paste options available?
   (a) File (b) Edit
   (c) View (d) None of these

3. An input device that captures text and pictures directly into the computer is known as
   (a) Keyboard (b) Microphone
   (c) Mouse (d) Scanner

4. Identify the icon shown in the image.

   (a) Control Panel (b) My Computer
   (c) Network (d) Recycle Bin

5. Which button should be clicked to reduce a window to a button on the taskbar?
   (a) Minimise (b) Maximise
   (c) Restore (d) Close

6. Output obtained on paper using a printer is called ....
   (a) Soft copy (b) Hard copy
   (c) Paper copy (d) None of these

7. The background of the desktop is called ....
   (a) Image   (b) Screen saver
   (c) Wallpaper   (d) None of these

8. You can change settings of your computer from the............. .
   (a) Recycle Bin   (b) Control Panel
   (c) Documents   (d) None of these

9. Which of these can contain files as well as folders?
   (a) Disk   (b) Screen saver
   (c) Drive   (d) None of these

10. If any file is deleted from a folder, it gets stored in ....
    (a) Control Panel   (b) Documents
    (c) Recycle Bin   (d) My Computer

11. 1 TB (Terabyte) is equal to ....
    (a) 100 GB   (b) 1000 GB   (c) 10 GB   (d) 10000 GB

12. .... is not a programming language.
    (a) HTML   (b) Java   (c) Python   (d) C++

13. Bit stands for ....
    (a) Binary Tree   (b) Bivariate Theory
    (c) Binary Digit   (d) None of these

14. Which memory card format is most widely used in smartphones?
    (a) Compact Flash (CF)   (b) Secure Digital (SD)
    (c) Smart Media   (d) Memory Stick

15. .... is a word processor which is used to type letters and make documents.
    (a) MS word   (b) Notepad
    (c) Wordpad   (d) All of these

16. The bar that contain menus of commands is called............. .
    (a) Menu bar   (b) Toolbar
    (c) Title bar   (d) All of these

17. What does a URL beginning with https:// indicates?
    (a) The webpage has free access to software.
    (b) You are visiting a secure website.
    (c) You are visiting an insecure website.
    (d) The webpage is deleting data to your browser.

18. Internet can be used for which of the following tasks?
(a) Buying and selling old and new goods
(b) Checking exam results
(c) Performing banking operations
(d) All of the above

19. The component of computer shown below is used for which purpose?

(a) Video calling   (b) Pointing on the screen
(c) Scanning a document   (d) Storing data

20. Which of the following requires large computer memory?
(a) Imaging   (b) Graphics
(c) Video   (d) All of these

21. The smallest unit of storage is.............. .
(a) Bit   (b) Byte   (c) Kilobyte   (d) Megabyte

22. What can you do using the Internet?
(a) Download software   (b) Participate in interactive forums
(c) Chat with your friends   (d) All of these

23. The tasks performed by Excel is similar to ....
(a) Word   (b) Powerpoint
(c) Microsoft Outlook   (d) Spreadsheet

24. Which of the following is not a web browser?
(a) Google Chrome   (b) Mozilla FireFox
(c) Internet Explorer   (d) Windows Explorer

25. Physical components of a computer which you can touch and feel are called ....
(a) Hardware   (b) Software
(c) Firmware   (d) Utility

26. Maximum zooming size available in Word Pad is ....
(a) 200   (b) 500
(c) 300   (d) 400

27. Who developed the World Wide Web?
(a) Sir Tim Berners-Lee   (b) Taub-Schilling
(c) Dennis Ritchie   (d) Donald Trump

28. The various parts of the computer are connected to each other with ....
(a) magnets   (b) power cables
(c) data cables   (d) None of these

29. Ctrl + X is used to ....
(a) select all document   (b) paste
(c) cut selected item   (d) None of these

30. The device shown in the image given below is used for which purpose?

(a) Playing games   (b) Flash light
(c) Reading Barcode   (d) None of these

Chapter 11

Scientists and Inventions

1. Who is the inventor of the Telephone?
   (a) Francis Beaufort
   (b) Henry Moseley
   (c) Alexander Graham Bell
   (d) Anthony Blatner

2. Who invented the Light Bulb?
   (a) Thomas Edison
   (b) Eli Whitney
   (c) Benjamin Franklin
   (d) Francis Beaufort

3. Who invented the Aeroplane?
   (a) The Wright brothers (Orville and Wilbur Wright)
   (b) James Watt
   (c) Thomas Edison
   (d) Galileo Galilei

4. .... invented the mobile phone.
   (a) Martin Cooper
   (b) Roger Bacon
   (c) Anthony Blatner
   (d) Thomas Edison

5. Who invented the ceiling fan?
   (a) Alexander Bereznyak
   (b) Philip Diehl
   (c) Charles Thermos
   (d) Rudolf Diesel

6. Which of the following instrument was invented by Galileo?
   (a) Barometer
   (b) Pendulum clock
   (c) Microscope
   (d) Thermometer

7. What Karl Benz invented?
   (a) The brake used in modern elevators
   (b) Jet Engine
   (c) Turbine
   (d) Motorcar

8. Which scientist discovered the radioactive element radium?
   (a) Isaac Newton
   (b) Albert Einstein
   (c) Benjamin Franklin
   (d) Marie Curie

9. Which Indian scientist won the Nobel prize for his contribution in field of Light Scattering?
   (a) Homi Bhabha　　(b) CV Raman　　(c) J. C. Bose　　(d) M.Visvesvaraya

10. Which Nuclear scientist of India is known as 'Father of Indian Nuclear Program'?
    (a) S.N. Bose　　(b) Homi Bhabha　　(c) Vikram Sarabhai　　(d) J. C. Bose

11. Who invented fountain pen?
    (a) Lewis Edson Waterman　　　　(b) Sir William Grove
    (c) Charles Kettering　　　　(d) George Fountain

12. The Father of White Revolution is ....
    (a) Patanjali　　　　(b) Jagadish Chandra Bose
    (c) Verghese Kurien　　　　(d) Raja Ramanna

13. The God particle Boson is named after which Indian scientist?
    (a) M. Visvesvaraya　　　　(b) Meghnad Saha
    (c) J. C. Bose　　　　(d) C. V. Raman

14. Identify the personality shown in the image.

Hint : He invented a reading and writing system for visually impaired people.
    (a) Thomas Alva Edison　　　　(b) Newton
    (c) Louis Braille　　　　(d) None of these

15. The first satellite of India shown in the image was named after which scientist?

    (a) Vikram Sarabhai　　　　(b) CV Raman
    (c) Aryabhatta　　　　(d) Sushutra

16. Identify the scientist shown in the image, who is known for inventing the Dynamite?

  (a) Michael Faraday   (b) Nicola Tesla
  (c) John Kepler   (d) Alfred Nobel

17. The scientist shown in the image invented the AC Motor, who is he?

  (a) Albert Einstein   (b) Michael Faraday
  (c) Nikola Tesla   (d) Isaac Newton

18. Which of the following instrument was invented by Sir Isaac Newton?
  (a) Reflecting telescope   (b) Chronometer
  (c) Microscope   (d) Spectacles

19. Which of the following scientists discovered that the Sun is the centre of the universe?
  (a) Hitler   (b) Nicolaus Copernicus
  (c) Galileo Galilei   (d) None of these

20. 'Pascal' is associated with which of the following invention?
  (a) Calculating Machine   (b) Barometer
  (c) Aeroplane   (d) Motor Car

First in India and World

1. Name the first country to make a Constitution.
   (a) India
   (b) United States of America
   (c) United Kingdom
   (d) France

2. Who was the first Indian woman to fly an aircraft?
   (a) K. Malleshwari
   (b) Kiran Mazumdar
   (c) Sarla Thakral
   (d) Harman Kaur

3. Who was the first woman to climb Mount Everest?
   (a) Arunima Sinha
   (b) Janet Yellen
   (c) Junko Tabei
   (d) Margaret Thatcher

4. Who is the first Indian woman to lead the flypast at Republic Day Parade of India?
   (a) Sakshi Malik
   (b) Depa Chand
   (c) Swati Rathore
   (d) None of these

5. Who was the first Indian to win Nobel Prize in Physics?
   (a) Rabindranath Tagore
   (b) C.V. Raman
   (c) Amartya Rathore
   (d) Dr Radhakrishnan

6. Who was the first Prime Minister of India?
   (a) VB Patel
   (b) Mahatma Gandhi
   (c) Rajendra Prasad
   (d) Jawaharlal Nehru

7. Name the first Indian bank.
   (a) Bank of Hindustan
   (b) Bank of Baroda
   (c) Reserve Bank of India
   (d) Punjab National Bank

8. Who is the first Indian to sail around the world?
   (a) Deepak Hooda
   (b) Abhilash Tomy
   (c) Bachendri Pal
   (d) Ashok Kumar

9. The first person to reach the space was ....
   (a) Rakesh Sharma
   (b) Yuri Gagarin
   (c) Alan Shepherd
   (d) Edwin Aldrin

10. Who was the first woman judge in Supreme Court of India?
    (a) Vijaya Laxmi Pandit
    (b) Fathima Beevi
    (c) Kamini Roy
    (d) Kadambini Ganguly

11. Who was the first Indian pilot?
    (a) Sardar Baldev Singh
    (b) J.R.D. Tata
    (c) Sardar Vallabh Bhai Patel
    (d) R.K. Shanmukham Chetty

12. Who was the first Indian woman to win Miss World contest?
    (a) Priyanka Chopra
    (b) Diana Hayden
    (c) Reita Faria
    (d) Aishwarya Rai

13. Name the First Indian to cross English channel.
    (a) Arati Saha
    (b) Amitabh Ghosh
    (c) Mihir Sen
    (d) Baldev Sahni

14. Who was the first woman Chief Minister in India?
    (a) Mamata Banerjee
    (b) Sushma Swaraj
    (c) Sucheta Kripalani
    (d) J. Jayalalithaa

15. Who was the first President of U.S.A?
    (a) George Washington
    (b) Robert Walpole
    (c) Donald Trump
    (d) Joe Biden

16. Who was the first Indian woman to receive Nobel Prize?
    (a) Indira Gandhi
    (b) Bachendri Pal
    (c) Mother Teresa
    (d) Aarti Saha

17. Who was the first Indian cricketer to score a Double century in ODI match?
    (a) Rohit Sharma
    (b) Virendra Sehwag
    (c) Sachin Tendulkar
    (d) M.S. Dhoni

18. Who became the first Indian pilot of Rafale Jet?
    (a) Abhinandan Rathore
    (b) Hilal Ahmed Rather
    (c) Rakesh Sharma
    (d) A. Chaturvedi

19. Name the first country to issue the paper currency.
    (a) India
    (b) USA
    (c) Australia
    (d) China

20. Who was the first Indian man to climb Mount Everest?
    (a) Avtar Singh
    (b) Neeraj Chopra
    (c) Mandip Singh
    (d) Love Raj

Books and Authors

1. Name the author of the book 'Wings of Fire'.
   (a) Narendra Modi
   (b) Jawaharlal Nehru
   (c) A. P. J. Abdul Kalam
   (d) None of these

2. Who wrote the book 'Arthashastra'?
   (a) Kautilya
   (b) Premchandra
   (c) Abul Fazal
   (d) Prakash Padukone

3. 'Playing It My Way' is the biography of ....
   (a) Virat Kohli
   (b) Sachin Tendulkar
   (c) Sunil Gavaskar
   (d) Milkha Singh

4. Who is the author of the book "The Diary of a Young Girl"?
   (a) Rachel Carson
   (b) Roland Barthes
   (c) Anne Frank
   (d) Ibn battuta

5. Who is the author of the book 'Playing to Win'?
   (a) Saina Nehwal
   (b) M.S. Dhoni
   (c) Rohit Sharma
   (d) Dutee Chand

6. Name the author of the book 'Broken Wings'.
   (a) Arunima Sinha
   (b) Premchand
   (c) Anne Frank
   (d) Sarojini Naidu

7. Which book is written by 'Kiran Bedi'?
   (a) It's Always Possible
   (b) My Country My Life
   (c) The Idea of Justice
   (d) Wings of Fire

8. Who wrote the book "Midnight's Children"?
   (a) Salman Rushdie
   (b) Milkha Singh
   (c) Narendra Modi
   (d) Helen Keller

9. Who is the author of the book 'The Race of My Life'?
   (a) Usain Bolt
   (b) Milkha Singh
   (c) Rudyard Kipling
   (d) Chetan Bhagat

10. Name the book written by 'Nelson Mandela'.
    (a) My Experiment with Truth   (b) Bunch of Old Letters
    (c) Godan   (d) Long Walk to Freedom

11. Who wrote the book 'The Story of My Life'?
    (a) Sarojini Naidu   (b) Helen Keller
    (c) William Shakespeare   (d) Michael Jackson

12. The book "I Do What I Do" is written by ....
    (a) Manmohan Singh   (b) Narendra Modi
    (c) Raghuram Rajan   (d) None of these

13. 'The Story of My Experiments with Truth' book is written by ....
    (a) Nelson Mandela   (b) Martin Luther King
    (c) Mahatma Gandhi   (d) Jawaharlal Nehru

14. 'All's Well That Ends Well' book is written by ....
    (a) Charles Dickens   (b) William Shakespeare
    (c) Abdul Kalam   (d) JK Rowling

15. Who is the author of the book 'Akbarnama'?
    (a) Akbar   (b) Babur
    (c) Abul Fazal   (d) Birbal

16. Who wrote the book 'Bunch of Old Letters'?
    (a) Indira Gandhi   (b) Rajiv Gandhi
    (c) Jawaharlal Nehru   (d) Motilal Nehru

17. The book 'Moonwalk' is written by ....
    (a) Charles Dickens   (b) Justin Bieber
    (c) William Shakespeare   (d) Michael Jackson

18. Who wrote the book 'Born Again on Mountain'?
    (a) Bachendri Pal   (b) Arunima Sinha
    (c) Junko Tabei   (d) None of these

Important Days and Dates

1. 'National Youth Day' is celebrated on which date?
   - (a) 15th January
   - (b) 9th January
   - (c) 18th January
   - (d) 12th January

2. 23rd January is celebrated as the birthday of ....
   - (a) Guru Govind Singh
   - (b) Subhash Chandra Bose
   - (c) Debendranath Tagore
   - (d) Chandra Shekhar Azad

3. The birthday of BR Ambedkar is celebrated on which date?
   - (a) 14th April
   - (b) 2nd May
   - (c) 5th April
   - (d) 8th June

4. On which date 'National Science Day' is celebrated?
   - (a) 5th May
   - (b) 15th March
   - (c) 5th January
   - (d) 28th February

5. When is National Sports Day celebrated in India?
   - (a) 29th August
   - (b) 4th May
   - (c) 17th September
   - (d) 5th July

6. When is 'Hindi Diwas' celebrated?
   - (a) 12th November
   - (b) 11th November
   - (c) 14th September
   - (d) 29th October

7. 'National Education Day' is celebrated on............... .
   - (a) 12th November
   - (b) 11th November
   - (c) 5th November
   - (d) 29th November

8. When is the 'Navy Day' celebrated every year in India?
   - (a) 29th December
   - (b) 4th December
   - (c) 10th December
   - (d) 12th January

9. 'World Water Conservation' Day is celebrated on which date?
   (a) 28th February
   (b) 22nd March
   (c) 5th June
   (d) 11th July

10. 'International Earth Day' is celebrated on which date?
   (a) 20th February
   (b) 21st March
   (c) 7th April
   (d) 22nd April

11. When is 'World Environment Day' celebrated?
   (a) 11th December
   (b) 20th December
   (c) 15th September
   (d) 5th June

12. 'Good Governance Day' is celebrated each year to mark the birth anniversary of ....
   (a) Sardar Patel
   (b) Indira Gandhi
   (c) Atal Bihari Vajpayee
   (d) Mahatma Gandhi

13. 'World Students Day' is celebrated on which date?
   (a) 17th November
   (b) 4th September
   (c) 9th December
   (d) 20th April

14. 25th January is celebrated as which day?
   (a) World Leprosy Eradication Day
   (b) Shaheed Diwas
   (c) National Tourism Day
   (d) World Day of the Handicapped

15. On which date the Constitution of India came into effect?
   (a) 24th January
   (b) 26th January
   (c) 31st January
   (d) None of these

16. 15th January is observed as........ .
   (a) Makar Sankranti
   (b) Indian Army Day
   (c) Indian Navy Day
   (d) Anti Terrorism Day

17. Match the following.

Days		Dates	
A.	Doctor's Day	1.	2nd Sunday of May
B.	Independence Day	2.	1st July
C.	Mother's Day	3.	15th August

Codes

	A	B	C			A	B	C
(a)	1	3	2		(b)	2	3	1
(c)	3	2	1		(d)	None of these		

Awards

1. Highest award that can be given to a civilian in India is ....
   (a) Bharat Ratna
   (b) Padma Vibhushan
   (c) Shravan Award
   (d) None of these

2. Who was the first Indian to get Nobel Prize in Physics?
   (a) Rabindranath Tagore
   (b) C.V. Raman
   (c) Amartya Sen
   (d) A.P.J. Abdul Kalam

3. Which of the following awards is the highest award in cinema given in India?
   (a) IIFA Award
   (b) Oscar Award
   (c) Filmfare Award
   (d) Dada Saheb Phalke Award

4. Which country awards the Nobel Prize?
   (a) Ireland
   (b) Sweden
   (c) England
   (d) America

5. Which is highest gallantry award for the personnel of Armed Forces in India?
   (a) Ashoka Chakra
   (b) Maha Vir Chakra
   (c) Param Vir Chakra
   (d) Kirti Chakra

6. The 'Dronacharya Award' is associated with ....
   (a) Eminent Surgeons
   (b) Famous Artists
   (c) Sport Coaches
   (d) Expert Engineers

7. Nobel Prizes are not given for which of the following fields?
   (a) Physics
   (b) Chemistry
   (c) Peace
   (d) Music

8. The Pulitzer Prize is associated with which one of the following?
   (a) Environmental protection
   (b) Olympic Games
   (c) Journalism
   (d) Civil Aviation

9. Who was the first Indian to receive a Nobel Prize?
   (a) Mother Teresa
   (b) Hargobind Tagore
   (c) CV Raman
   (d) Rabindranath Tagore

10. Which of the following is not an award in the field of literature?

(a) Sahitya Akademi Award

(b) Jnanpith Award

(c) Padma Shri

(d) Saraswati Samman

11. Which of the following awards is associated with performance in T.V. industry?

(a) Academy Award

(b) BAFTA Award

(c) Emmy Award

(d) Golden Globe Award

12. Which of the following organisations/states awards the Vyas Samman and Saraswati Samman in the field of literature?

(a) Madhya Pradesh

(b) KK Birla Foundation

(c) Tata Education and Development Trust

(d) Uttar Pradesh

13. Arjuna Award is given for ....

(a) bravery on battlefield

(b) outstanding performance in sports

(c) exceptional service in emergency

(d) exceptional service to slum dwellers

14. Marie Curie was awarded Nobel Prize twice in the fields of ....

(a) Physics and Chemistry

(b) Chemistry and Medicine

(c) Physics and Medicine

(d) Chemistry and Peace

15. 'Academy Awards' are also known as ....

(a) Oscar Awards

(b) Golden Globe Awards

(c) Pulitzer Prize

(d) Man Booker Prize

16. Booker Prize is given in the field of ....

(a) Medicine

(b) Adventure

(c) Fiction writing

(d) Science

17. Who was the first Indian woman to win 'Miss Universe' contest?

(a) Priyanka Chopra

(b) Sushmita Sen

(c) Madhuri Dixit

(d) Manushi Chhillar

18. Who was the first person to receive Bharat Ratna Award?

(a) Dr Radhakrishnan

(b) Indira Gandhi

(c) Mahatma Gandhi

(d) Sardar Vallabhbhai Patel

19. Nobel prize is given in how many fields?

(a) 5

(b) 6

(c) 7

(d) 8

Chapter

16

Sports

1. Abhinav Bindra won India's first individual Olympic gold medal in ....
   (a) archery (b) shooting
   (c) wrestling (d) boxing

2. Which of the following is not a team sport in Olympics?
   (a) Water Polo (b) Handball
   (c) Judo (d) Basketball

3. Dipa Karmakar is associated with the sport of ....
   (a) Gymnastics (b) Judo
   (c) Taekwondo (d) Shooting

4. Which of the following term is used in cricket?
   (a) Smash (b) LBW
   (c) Scoop (d) Kick

5. Back Flip : Gymnastic :: .... : Swimming.
   (a) Flag kick (b) Knock out
   (c) LBW (d) Butterfly

6. Identify the Indian Olympian and tennis player shown in the image.

   (a) Mahesh Bhupathi (b) Rohan Bopanna
   (c) Leander Paes (d) Yuki Bhambhri

7. Tiger woods is associated with which sport?
   (a) Golf (b) Hockey
   (c) Polo (d) Badminton

8. Who is the Indian Sprinter shown in the image below?

(a) PT Usha   (b) Rita Sen   (c) Neelu Mishra   (d) Hima Das

9. Identify the sport symbol shown in the image.

(a) Shooting   (b) Cycling   (c) Swimming   (d) Archery

10. Match the List I with List II.

	List I		List II
A.	Grand Slam	1.	Chess
B.	Grand Prix	2.	Formula One Racing
C.	Grand Master	3.	Tennis

Codes

	A	B	C			A	B	C
(a)	2	1	3		(b)	3	2	1
(c)	1	2	3		(d)	2	3	1

11. Which of the following term is related with the game of Hockey?
(a) Follow on   (b) Tie breaker   (c) Hat trick   (d) Half Volley

12. "Narendra Modi" cricket stadium is situated in ....
(a) Ahmedabad   (b) Surat
(c) Vadodara   (d) Rajkot

13. How many players are their in each team of baseball?
(a) 11   (b) 8   (c) 9   (d) 10

14. Which of the following is not a type of aerobic exercise?
(a) Swimming   (b) Running   (c) Talking   (d) Walking

15. Identify the player shown in the image.

(a) Virendar Sehwag   (b) Virat Kohli
(c) Kapil Dev   (d) Rohit Sharma

16. Which player is also known as "Golden Girl"?
(a) Saina Nehwal   (b) PV Sindhu
(c) PT Usha   (d) None of these

17. Match List I with List II.

	List I (Sportsperson)		**List II** (Sport)
A.	PV Sindhu	1.	Shooting
B.	Manu Bhaker	2.	Boxing
C.	Mary Kom	3.	Badminton

Codes

	A	B	C			A	B	C
(a)	3	1	2		(b)	2	3	1
(c)	1	3	2		(d)	1	2	3

18. Match List I with List II.

	List I (Countries)		**List II** (National/Popular games)
A.	Pakistan	1.	Cricket
B.	England	2.	Golf
C.	Scotland	3.	Field hockey
D.	New Zealand	4.	Rugby union

Codes

	A	B	C	D			A	B	C	D
(a)	2	3	4	1		(b)	3	1	2	4
(c)	1	3	4	2		(d)	4	2	3	1

PRACTICE SET 01

1. Which of the following connects the Brain with other parts of the body?
   (a) Heart   (b) Spinal Cord   (c) Bones   (d) Tendons

2. 'National Unity Day' is celebrated on the birth anniversary of which leader?
   (a) Atal Bihari Vajpayee   (b) Jawaharlal Nehru
   (c) Mahatma Gandhi   (d) Sardar Patel

3. Who among the following win the Nobel Prize in two fields?
   (a) Maria Goeppert-Mayer   (b) Marie Curie
   (c) Dorothy Crowfoot Hodgkin   (d) Barbara McClintock

4. Chennai is the capital of which state?
   (a) Kerala   (b) Tamil Nadu   (c) Karnataka   (d) Maharashtra

5. The dance shown in the image is practised in which state?

   (a) Manipur   (b) Haryana   (c) Gujarat   (d) Uttar Pradesh

6. Who is considered as the founder of E-mail?
   (a) Bill Gates   (b) Jeff Bezos   (c) Ray Tomlinson   (d) Steve Jobs

7. Sun is made up of which gases?
   (a) Carbon dioxide and Oxygen   (b) Hydrogen and Helium
   (c) Nitrogen and Carbon dioxide   (d) Helium and Sulphur

8. Which of the following term is used in Basketball?
   (a) Smash   (b) LBW   (c) Free Throw   (d) Kick

9. Sound can travel through, which of the following medium?
   (a) Iron Rod   (b) Brick Wall   (c) Wooden Block   (d) All of these

10. Who was the first Indian to get Nobel Prize in Economics?
    (a) Rabindranath Tagore   (b) CV Raman
    (c) Amartya Sen   (d) A.P.J. Abdul Kalam

11. The famous Novel Idgah is written by which Indian novelist?
    (a) Mahadevi Varma   (b) Premchand
    (c) Suryakant Tripathi   (d) Harivansh Rai Bachchan

12. What is the meaning of term 'V' in DVD?
    (a) Visual   (b) Virtual   (c) Versatile   (d) Various

13. What is the currency of Iraq?
    (a) Riyal   (b) Dinar   (c) Yen   (d) Euro

14. Badrinath is situated on the bank of river ....
    (a) Krishna   (b) Yamuna   (c) Alaknanda   (d) Saraswati

15. Which was the first successful mission to Planet Mars?
    (a) Mangalyan   (b) Mariner   (c) Apollo   (d) Polka

16. Which of the following is not a green house gas?
    (a) Carbon dioxide   (b) Methane
    (c) Nitrous oxide   (d) Carbon monoxide

17. Chess : Indoors :: .... : Outdoors.
    (a) Ludo   (b) Carrom   (c) Cards   (d) Basketball

18. Earth completes one .... in 365 days.
    (a) revolution   (b) spinning   (c) circulation   (d) rotation

19. The battery used in Automobiles and mobile phones was invented by which scientist?
    (a) Thomas Edison   (b) Allesandro Volta   (c) Nikola Tesla   (d) Isaac Newton

20. Name the highest mountain peak in India.
    (a) Mount Everest   (b) Kanchenjunga   (c) Nanda Devi   (d) None of these

21. Which is the oldest musical instrument of India?
    (a) Flute   (b) Tabla   (c) Veena   (d) Sitar

22. Where is "Jim Corbett National Park" located?
    (a) Arunachal Pradesh   (b) Bihar
    (c) Uttar Pradesh   (d) Uttarakhand

23. Which of the following is not a computer program?
    (a) Internet Browser   (b) MS Word   (c) Android   (d) Notepad

24. Identify the personality shown in the image.

(a) President of Australia
(b) Vice-President of USA
(c) President of New Zealand
(d) Prime Minister of Sri Lanka

25. 'National Sports Day' is celebrated on the Birth Anniversary of which great sports person?
(a) Milkha SIngh
(b) Dhyan Chand
(c) Sachin Tendulkar
(d) PT Usha

26. Which mineral helps in strengthening the Enamel in Human tooth?
(a) Copper (b) Calcium (c) Iron (d) None of these

27. The personality shown in the picture is the author of the book 'Two States'. Who is He?

(a) Kanishk Tharoor
(b) Aditya Gautam
(c) Chetan Bhagat
(d) Amish Tripathi

28. The famous Jagannath temple is located in which state of India?
(a) Uttar Pradesh (b) Maharashtra (c) Odisha (d) Andhra Pradesh

29. The speed of Ships is measured in which unit?
(a) Kilometer (b) Knot (c) Pascal (d) Kelvin

30. Which is highest gallantry award for the personnel of Armed forces in India?
(a) Ashoka Chakra
(b) Maha Vir Chakra
(c) Param Vir Chakra
(d) Kirti Chakra

31. Match List I with List II.

	List I (Country)		**List II** (Capital)
A.	Russia	1.	Burma
B.	Myanmar	2.	Islamabad
C.	Pakistan	3.	Brasilia
D.	Brazil	4.	Moscow

Codes

	A	B	C	D			A	B	C	D
(a)	4	3	2	1		(b)	3	2	4	1
(c)	2	3	1	4		(d)	4	1	2	3

32. Which of the given statement is correct?

Statement 1 The oldest religious book in the world is Rig Veda.
Statement 2 Monastries are religious places associated with Sikhism.

Codes
(a) Only 1 is true (b) Only 2 is true (c) Both 1 and 2 are true (d) None of these

33. Match the List I with List II

	List I (State)		**List II** (Capital)
A.	Madhya Pradesh	1.	Shillong
B.	Odisha	2.	Thiruvananthapuram
C.	Meghalaya	3.	Bhopal
D.	Kerala	4.	Bhubaneswar

Codes

	A	B	C	D			A	B	C	D
(a)	1	3	2	4		(b)	3	4	1	2
(c)	4	1	2	3		(d)	4	3	2	1

34. Who is the founder of Chinese e-commerce company 'Alibaba'?
(a) Elon Musk (b) Bill Gates (c) Jack Ma (d) Steve Jobs

35. The Monument shown in the image is located in which city?

(a) New York (b) Sydney (c) Mumbai (d) Riyadh

PRACTICE SET 02

1. Which of the following is the winter capital of Uttarakhand?
   (a) Shimla (b) Dehradun (c) Srinagar (d) Manali

2. Dribble : Basketball :: .... :Tennis
   (a) Flip Shot (b) Long Kick (c) Forehand (d) Butterfly

3. In the image shown below, the Earth is rotating on its ....

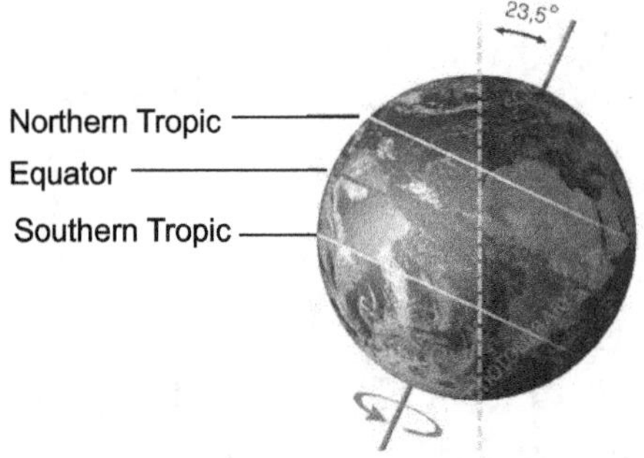

   (a) Orbit (b) Axis (c) Path (d) Line

4. The first Quartz Clock of the world was invented by ______
   (a) P. Spencer (b) Warren Marrison
   (c) Willis Carrier (d) Leonardo Da Vinci

5. Which of the following city is not located along the River Ganga?
   (a) Varanasi (b) Patna (c) Kanpur (d) Vadodara

6. Which folk dance is shown in the image given below?

   (a) Bhangra (b) Bihu dance (c) Giddha (d) Dandiya

7. Aizawl is the capital of which state of India?

   (a) Arunachal Pradesh   (b) Tamil Nadu

   (c) Mizoram   (d) Assam

8. What is the name of the American Leader shown in the image?

   (a) Benjamin Franklin (b) Abraham Lincoln   (c) Martin Luther King   (d) George Bush

9. Which day is celebrated in India to salute the soldiers who sacrificed their lives to protect the country?

   (a) Independence Day (b) National Peace Day (c) Army Day   (d) Martyr's Day

10. Which part of the body filters the blood and removes the wastes from the body?

   (a) Lungs   (b) Kidneys   (c) Stomach   (d) Heart

11. The clock tower shown in the image is located in which country?

   (a) United States of America   (b) United Kingdom

   (c) China   (d) Australia

12. The national currency of France is ....

   (a) Franc   (b) Baht   (c) Pound   (d) Lira

13. Which of the following is not a Web Browser?

   (a) Safari   (b) Chrome   (c) Firefox   (d) Adobe

14. "The Cat in the Hat" is one of the greatest children's books written by ....

   (a) A. A. Milne   (b) Dr. Seuss   (c) T. S. Eliot   (d) Maurice Sendak

15. Which is the second highest civilian award of India?
(a) Bharat Ratna (b) Param Vir Chakra (c) Padma Vibhushan (d) Arjun Award

16. Identify the substance that does not get dissolved in water.
(a) Oil (b) Oxygen (c) Water (d) Sugar

17. Free Kick: Football:: Yorker: ....
(a) Baseball (b) Cricket (c) Hockey (d) Javelin Throw

18. Which of the following heavenly bodies is also known as fossil planet?
(a) Earth (b) Sun (c) Moon (d) Asteroid

19. Who discovered the Human Cell?
(a) Robert Hooke (b) Gregor Mendel (c) Charles Darwin (d) None of these

20. Which gas protects the Biosphere from harmful UV Radiations?
(a) Carbon dioxide (b) Ozone (c) Nitrogen (d) Sulphur

21. 'Madhubani', a style of folk paintings, is popular in which of the following states in India?
(a) Uttar Pradesh (b) Rajasthan (c) Madhya Pradesh (d) Bihar

22. Which of the following is known as The City of Oranges?
(a) Jaipur (b) Delhi (c) Nagpur (d) Chennai

23. Steve Jobs and Steve Wozniak are the founder of which multinational company?
(a) Apple (b) Microsoft (c) Adobe (d) SamSung

24. The Birth Anniversary of which Indian leader is celebrated as 'Good Governance Day'?
(a) Sardar Vallabhbhai Patel (b) Jawaharlal Nehru
(c) Atal Bihari Vajpayee (d) Indira Gandhi

25. What is the function of Tendon in the Human body?
(a) Connects Brain to Heart (b) Connects Bone to Bone
(c) Connects Muscles to Bone (d) Connects Fingers with Arm

26. Which was the first Indian bank?
(a) Bank of Hindustan (b) Bank of Baroda
(c) Reserve Bank of India (d) Punjab National Bank

27. Mecca and Medina, the Holy sites of Islam are located in which country?
(a) United Arab Emirates (b) Saudi Arabia (c) Turkey (d) Pakistan

28. .... is the national currency of Russia.
(a) Dollar (b) Rubble (c) Peso (d) Euro

29. Which of the following is a storage device?
 (a) Compact Disk (b) Flash Drive (c) Floppy Disk (d) All of these

30. The Book 'The Test of My Life' is the Biography of which Indian Cricketer?
 (a) Sachin Tendulkar (b) Kapil Dev (c) Yuvraj Singh (d) MS Dhoni

31. Which of the following nutrient is good for strong bones?
 1. Vitamin D   2. Vitamin K   3. Calcium

 Codes
 (a) Only 1 (b) Only 2 and 3 (c) Only 1 and 3 (d) All of these

32. Match the List I with List II.

	List I (Day)		**List II** (Date)
A.	Doctor's Day	1.	5th June
B.	World Food Day	2.	1st July
C.	World Environment Day	3.	16th October

 Codes

	A	B	C			A	B	C
(a)	1	3	2		(b)	2	3	1
(c)	3	2	1		(d)	1	2	3

33. Which of the given pairs are matched correctly?

	Country		**Capital**
A.	Australia	—	Canberra
B.	Cabada	—	New York
C.	Egypt	—	Cairo

 Codes
 (a) Only 1 and 2 (b) Only 2 and 3
 (c) Only 1 and 3 (d) All of these

34. The first computer of the world was built by.................... .
 (a) Alan Turing (b) Charles Babbage (c) Steve Woznaik (d) None of these

35. Who among the following painters was the first one to draw the painting of Bharat Mata?
 (a) MF Hussain (b) Abanindra Nath Tagore
 (c) Raja Ravi Verma (d) Nanda Lal Bose

Answers

Chapter 1   Solar System

1. (a)	**2.** (d)	**3.** (c)	**4.** (d)	**5.** (d)	**6.** (d)	**7.** (c)	**8.** (d)	**9.** (a)	**10.** (b)
11. (d)	**12.** (a)	**13.** (a)	**14.** (b)	**15.** (a)	**16.** (a)	**17.** (d)	**18.** (d)	**19.** (b)	**20.** (c)
21. (c)	**22.** (c)	**23.** (b)	**24.** (c)	**25.** (d)	**26.** (a)	**27.** (a)	**28.** (a)	**29.** (c)	**30.** (c)

Chapter 2   My Country

1. (c)	**2.** (a)	**3.** (d)	**4.** (d)	**5.** (a)	**6.** (a)	**7.** (c)	**8.** (c)	**9.** (d)	**10.** (c)
11. (c)	**12.** (d)	**13.** (d)	**14.** (b)	**15.** (b)	**16.** (a)	**17.** (b)	**18.** (b)	**19.** (a)	**20.** (b)
21. (c)	**22.** (c)	**23.** (c)	**24.** (d)	**25.** (c)					

Chapter 3   Famous Buildings and Monuments

1. (d)	**2.** (c)	**3.** (d)	**4.** (c)	**5.** (c)	**6.** (b)	**7.** (d)	**8.** (b)	**9.** (b)	**10.** (d)
11. (a)	**12.** (b)	**13.** (b)	**14.** (a)	**15.** (c)	**16.** (a)	**17.** (c)	**18.** (a)	**19.** (a)	**20.** (a)
21. (c)	**22.** (d)	**23.** (d)	**24.** (a)	**25.** (a)					

Chapter 4   Our Culture

1. (c)	**2.** (c)	**3.** (b)	**4.** (d)	**5.** (a)	**6.** (b)	**7.** (d)	**8.** (c)	**9.** (c)	**10.** (b)
11. (b)	**12.** (b)	**13.** (c)	**14.** (c)	**15.** (d)	**16.** (a)	**17.** (d)	**18.** (c)	**19.** (a)	**20.** (d)
21. (c)	**22.** (c)	**23.** (c)							

Chapter 5   Capital and Currencies

1. (d)	**2.** (a)	**3.** (c)	**4.** (a)	**5.** (c)	**6.** (b)	**7.** (a)	**8.** (b)	**9.** (c)	**10.** (b)
11. (c)	**12.** (a)	**13.** (d)	**14.** (c)	**15.** (d)	**16.** (b)	**17.** (a)	**18.** (b)	**19.** (d)	**20.** (a)
21. (a)	**22.** (a)	**23.** (c)	**24.** (d)	**25.** (c)					

Chapter 6   International Personalities

1. (b)	**2.** (c)	**3.** (b)	**4.** (a)	**5.** (b)	**6.** (c)	**7.** (a)	**8.** (c)	**9.** (c)	**10.** (c)
11. (a)	**12.** (a)	**13.** (a)	**14.** (b)	**15.** (d)	**16.** (a)	**17.** (b)	**18.** (a)	**19.** (a)	**20.** (b)

Chapter 7   Our Environment

1. (c)	2. (d)	3. (b)	4. (b)	5. (d)	6. (d)	7. (d)	8. (d)	9. (d)	10. (d)
11. (d)	12. (b)	13. (c)	14. (a)	15. (b)	16. (d)	17. (b)	18. (c)	19. (b)	20. (c)
21. (d)	22. (b)	23. (a)	24. (a)	25. (d)					

Chapter 8   Human Body

1. (c)	2. (b)	3. (b)	4. (c)	5. (d)	6. (c)	7. (a)	8. (b)	9. (d)	10. (d)
11. (c)	12. (c)	13. (b)	14. (c)	15. (a)	16. (c)	17. (d)	18. (d)	19. (c)	20. (b)
21. (a)	22. (b)	23. (a)	24. (a)	25. (b)	26. (b)	27. (a)	28. (b)	29. (c)	30. (a)
31. (d)									

Chapter 9   Everyday Science

1. (d)	2. (c)	3. (b)	4. (a)	5. (a)	6. (a)	7. (a)	8. (d)	9. (c)	10. (a)
11. (a)	12. (b)	13. (c)	14. (d)	15. (c)	16. (a)	17. (a)	18. (a)	19. (a)	20. (b)

Chapter 10   Computers

1. (a)	2. (b)	3. (d)	4. (d)	5. (a)	6. (b)	7. (c)	8. (b)	9. (c)	10. (c)
11. (b)	12. (a)	13. (c)	14. (b)	15. (d)	16. (a)	17. (b)	18. (d)	19. (d)	20. (d)
21. (a)	22. (d)	23. (d)	24. (d)	25. (a)	26. (b)	27. (a)	28. (c)	29. (c)	30. (c)

Chapter 11   Scientists and Inventions

1. (c)	2. (a)	3. (a)	4. (a)	5. (b)	6. (d)	7. (d)	8. (d)	9. (b)	10. (b)
11. (a)	12. (c)	13. (c)	14. (c)	15. (c)	16. (d)	17. (c)	18. (a)	19. (b)	20. (a)

Chapter 12   First in India and World

1. (b)	2. (c)	3. (c)	4. (c)	5. (b)	6. (d)	7. (a)	8. (b)	9. (b)	10. (b)
11. (b)	12. (c)	13. (c)	14. (c)	15. (a)	16. (c)	17. (c)	18. (b)	19. (d)	20. (a)

Chapter 13   Books and Authors

1. (c)	2. (a)	3. (b)	4. (c)	5. (a)	6. (d)	7. (a)	8. (a)	9. (b)	10. (d)
11. (b)	12. (c)	13. (c)	14. (b)	15. (c)	16. (c)	17. (d)	18. (b)		

Chapter 14   Important Days and Dates

1. (d)	**2.** (b)	**3.** (a)	**4.** (d)	**5.** (a)	**6.** (c)	**7.** (b)	**8.** (b)	**9.** (b)	**10.** (d)
11. (d)	**12.** (c)	**13.** (a)	**14.** (c)	**15.** (b)	**16.** (b)	**17.** (b)			

Chapter 15   Awards

1. (a)	**2.** (b)	**3.** (d)	**4.** (b)	**5.** (c)	**6.** (c)	**7.** (d)	**8.** (c)	**9.** (d)	**10.** (c)
11. (c)	**12.** (b)	**13.** (b)	**14.** (a)	**15.** (a)	**16.** (c)	**17.** (b)	**18.** (a)	**19.** (b)	

Chapter 16   Sports

1. (b)	**2.** (c)	**3.** (a)	**4.** (b)	**5.** (d)	**6.** (c)	**7.** (a)	**8.** (d)	**9.** (d)	**10.** (b)
11. (b)	**12.** (a)	**13.** (c)	**14.** (c)	**15.** (a)	**16.** (c)	**17.** (a)	**18.** (b)		

Practice Set 1

1. (b)	**2.** (d)	**3.** (b)	**4.** (b)	**5.** (c)	**6.** (c)	**7.** (b)	**8.** (c)	**9.** (d)	**10.** (c)
11. (b)	**12.** (c)	**13.** (b)	**14.** (c)	**15.** (b)	**16.** (d)	**17.** (d)	**18.** (a)	**19.** (b)	**20.** (b)
21. (c)	**22.** (d)	**23.** (c)	**24.** (b)	**25.** (b)	**26.** (b)	**27.** (c)	**28.** (c)	**29.** (b)	**30.** (c)
31. (d)	**32.** (a)	**33.** (b)	**34.** (c)	**35.** (b)					

Practice Set 2

1. (b)	**2.** (c)	**3.** (b)	**4.** (b)	**5.** (d)	**6.** (c)	**7.** (c)	**8.** (c)	**9.** (c)	**10.** (b)
11. (b)	**12.** (a)	**13.** (d)	**14.** (b)	**15.** (c)	**16.** (a)	**17.** (b)	**18.** (c)	**19.** (a)	**20.** (b)
21. (d)	**22.** (c)	**23.** (a)	**24.** (c)	**25.** (c)	**26.** (a)	**27.** (b)	**28.** (b)	**29.** (d)	**30.** (c)
31. (c)	**32.** (b)	**33.** (c)	**34.** (b)	**35.** (b)